Fluffy and the Rainbow in his Heart

Creator and illustrator: Patrick Arguin

English translation: Bleu Dactylo

French version written by: Michèle Rappe
Support, coaching and collaboration: Hélène Beaudette

I want to offer my deepest gratitude to Hélène Beaudette.
Her unconditional support and presence allowed TOOLS OF THE HEART to grow and come into form.

Father Sun and Mother Earth have created
a beautiful garden that they deeply love.
Their hearts are filled with joy.

However, from time to time, areas of shade were seen in some parts of the garden. Father Sun and Mother Earth could feel the sadness.

«How can I help my garden find its smile back?» worries Mother Earth.

«I asked our friend the Moon for some advice,» says Father Sun. «I will take care of it.»

Father Sun scans the garden when suddenly, he hears a little squirrel crying. «Hello Fluffy, why are you crying?» asks Father Sun.

«I am sad, and I feel all alone,» says the squirrel, «everything seems grey!»

«Oh! It's true that sadness often looks like big dark clouds,» replies Father Sun, «but did you know that there is a beautiful rainbow in your heart?»

Fluffy is puzzled. «How can there be a rainbow in my heart?» he asks.

«Come with me,» says Father Sun. «Let's find a calmer place, and I will tell you how to find it.»

Fluffy sat near a waterfall to listen to Father Sun talk about the rainbow.

Comfortably seated, he could hear the water flowing softly, and he closed his eyes.

«First of all,» says Father Sun, «inhale slowly while gently feeling your belly go out. Then, exhale slowly.»

«Again, Inhale, hmffffffffffff. Exhale, pffffffffffff.»

Fluffy takes several slow and deep breaths.

Fluffy feels much more calm.
An orange elf appears before him and kindly addresses him.

«Imagine yourself at the top of a staircase,» says Orange.
«Go down the stairs slowly.»
7... 6.... 5..... 4...... 3....... 2.......1
«There, in front of you, is a door and we will open it together to discover a wonderful place.»

The squirrel feels good, and carefully listens to the elf. «Now,» says Orange, «imagine you arrive in a wonderful garden.»

There are beautiful trees, colorful flowers, and a peaceful river. «Look at all those wonders before you!»

Fluffy goes on to discover other parts of the garden with the elf. He is taking his time to enjoy it as much as he can.

Then, Orange shows him the beautiful rainbow Father Sun told him about.

A beautiful orange light surrounds the squirrel.
He feels a lot of softness; just like the love of Mother Earth.

Orange then says to Fluffy;
«Anytime you feel like it; you can go
down these stairs again to come to this
wonderful place.»

«The light of your rainbow of wisdom
will help you push away the dark clouds.
Even if you cannot see it, this light is
always there in your heart.»

Father Sun gently caresses Fluffy who slowly opens his eyes. The clouds are gone!

«Tell me Father Sun, what is wisdom?»
«It is when you listen and trust what is inside your heart. But sometimes you need help, that is why the elves are there to guide you.»

Father Sun bids farewell to Fluffy and continues to stroll in the garden. His visit makes the shadier parts sunny again. They learn how going inside your heart can help you find your well-being.

That night, before going to bed, Fluffy thinks about the elf. He also thinks about the love of Mother Earth and Father Sun. Treasured by the Moon, the garden echoes with laughter and cries of joy.

Remember...

How can I find my joy?
When you take the time to meditate and go inside your heart to find your rainbow of wisdom, it helps you push away the clouds of sadness. Joy then reappears, like the sun after the rain.

What can I do if my sadness does not go away?
If sadness stays inside you for too long or comes back too often, share your feelings with an adult you can trust and who will listen to you.

Can meditation work for me even if I do not feel sad?
Whenever you feel the need to calm down, take a moment to close your eyes and meditate, wherever you are. You can also meditate for the simple joy of feeling good!

The Book Collection

Tools of the Heart
Fostering Confidence and Self-esteem

1 **Father Sun and Mother Earth Create Life**
Breathing/Finding your rhythm
Breathing is essential to life; conscious breathing is a simple, yet effective way to regain your calm and well-being by finding your body's rhythm.

2 **Fluffy and the Rainbow in his Heart**
Meditation/Finding your inner calm
Each one of us has a peaceful place inside their heart. Meditation is a tool that allows you to find your personal space or to go back to it.

3 **Colin Discovers Confidence**
Grounding/Strengthening your self-confidence
Growing up often comes with its share of fears and hesitations. Growing solid roots helps to build and nurture a positive self-confidence.

4 **Colin and Fluffy Become Friends**
Knowing yourself/Loving and appreciating
Positive self-confidence and self-esteem are the building blocks of healthy relationships; therefore, learning to appreciate who we are is a treasure for life.

5 **The Choice**
Insight/Listening to your intuition
Learning to listen to your inner voice and how to trust it, is learning to stay true to yourself in all situations.

6 **Colin's Courage**
Expressing/Confidence in yourself
Standing up for yourself is not wrong. It is about relying on your self-worth with confidence, to respectfully say what you need to say.

7 **Enough is Enough**
Self-respect/Daring to be yourself
Developing good communication skills also implies expressing your feelings and needs in a respectful manner, which can sometimes be a challenge!

8 **Fluffy Finds his Well-being**
Self-awareness/Taking responsibility
Growing up is also about becoming more aware of your emotions and learning to manage them responsibly.

The Meditation Collection

Tools of the Heart
Fostering Confidence and Self-esteem

Specially designed for young children, the guided meditations explore and develop the same themes, as seen in the **Tools of the Heart** book collection. These intend to reinforce the children's knowledge of themselves through their inner space of wisdom, where things can be seen, heard, and felt.

Meditation is also a wonderful tool that children can easily learn to help them self-regulate physically, mentally, and emotionally.

To learn more, go to our website:
www.toolsoftheheart.com

www.ingramcontent.com/pod-product-compliance
Lightning Source LLC
Chambersburg PA
CBHW041158120626
46547CB00020B/3259